TWICKENHAM AND KINGSTON TRAMWAYS

Robert J Harley

MP Middleton Press

Cover Picture: Car 252 of the London United Tramways enters the single track in Victoria Road, Surbiton. This scene dates from about 1908 and the tramcar is resplendent in royal blue and white livery. This particular tram was later sold to Erith.

Cover Colours: These represent the red and white livery applied to LUT trams.

FEATURES IN LONDON TRAMWAY CLASSICS

Rolling Stock	Title
A class. LCC	Southwark and Deptford
A type MET	Waltham Cross and Edmonton
Alexandra Palace Elec. Rly.	Enfield and Wood Green
B class. LCC/Bexley	Greenwich and Dartford
B type MET	Stamford Hill
Barking cars	Ilford and Barking
Bexley cars	Greenwich and Dartford
Bluebird. LCC car 1	Camberwell and West Norwood
C class. LCC	Victoria and Lambeth
Cable cars	Clapham and Streatham
Croydon cars	Croydon's Tramways
C type MET/LT	Barnet and Finchley
D class. LCC	Wandsworth and Battersea
D type MET	Edgware and Willesden
Dartford cars	Greenwich and Dartford
East Ham cars	East Ham and West Ham
Erith cars	Greenwich and Dartford
E class. LCC/LT	Aldgate and Stepney
E1 class. LCC/LT	Lewisham and Catford
E1 cars 552-601. LCC/LT	Hampstead and Highgate
E1 cars 1777 -1851 LCC/LT	Clapham and Streatham
E3 class. LCC/LT	Camberwell and West Norwood
E3 class. Leyton/LT	Walthamstow and Leyton
E type MET/LT	Enfield and Wood Green
Experimental Tramcars MET/LUT/LT	Barnet and Finchley
F class. LCC	Embankment and Waterloo
F type MET	Waltham Cross and Edmonton
G class. LCC	Embankment and Waterloo
G type MET/LT	Stamford Hill
Gravesend & Northfleet cars	North Kent
H class (works). LCC/LT	Eltham and Woolwich
H type MET/LT	Stamford Hill
Horse cars. North Met./LCC	Aldgate and Stepney
HR2 class. LCC/LT	Camberwell and W Norwood
Ilford cars	Ilford and Barking
K class (works) LCC/LT	Waltham Cross and Edmonton
L class (works). LCC/LT	Holborn and Finsbury
L/1 class (works) LCC/LT	Clapham and Streatham
Leyton cars	Walthamstow and Leyton
LT car 2	Wandsworth and Battersea
LUT car 341	Kingston and Wimbledon
LUT Luxury Cars 175 and 275	Twickenham and Kingston
M class LCC/LT	Greenwich and Dartford
Petrol electric cars. LCC	Southwark and Deptford
SMET cars	Croydon's Tramways
S2 type LUT	Shepherds Bush and Uxbridge
T type LUT	Kingston and Wimbledon
Trailer cars LCC	Clapham and Streatham
UCC type MET/LT	Edgware and Willesden
U type LUT	Hammersmith and Hounslow
Walthamstow cars	Walthamstow and Leyton
West Ham cars	East Ham and West Ham
Works cars MET	Waltham Cross and Edmonton
Works cars LUT	Hammersmith and Hounslow
X type LUT	Shepherds Bush and Uxbridge
Z type LUT	Twickenham and Kingston

Miscellaneous

Accidents	Twickenham and Kingston
Advertising on tramcars	Aldgate and Stepney
Conduit system	Embankment and Waterloo
Overhead wiring	Edgware and Willesden
Power supply	Walthamstow and Leyton
Request stops	Victoria and Lambeth
Section boxes	Eltham and Woolwich
Staff Uniforms	Twickenham and Kingston
Track layouts - single & loops	Stamford Hill
Track Construction and Maintenance	Barnet and Finchley
Tram tours	Holborn and Finsbury
Upstairs - Downstairs	Hammersmith and Hounslow

First Published October 1999

ISBN 1 901706 35 4

© Middleton Press, 1999

Design Deborah Esher
       David Pede

Published by
       Middleton Press
       Easebourne Lane
       Midhurst, West Sussex
       GU29 9AZ
Tel: 01730 813169
Fax: 01730 812601

Printed & bound by Biddles Ltd,
       Guildford and Kings Lynn

CONTENTS

INTRODUCTION AND ACKNOWLEDGEMENTS

It is with some sadness that we come to the end of our *Tramway Classics* series on London. I would like to think that the 25 volumes covering the metropolitan area will have encouraged many readers to enquire further about their locality and the history of its public transport system. I extend my thanks to all those who have helped in this enterprise. My aims throughout have been to inform and bring pleasure to readers by presenting them with interesting views which otherwise might have lain unseen out of sight of the general public.

The trams of London were used by ordinary working people and their memory belongs to all of us.

I am deeply indebted to those who have lent views from their collections. Photos in this volume are from C.Carter, Curly Cross, A.D.Packer, John Gent, John Gillham, George Gundry and Dave Jones. I am also grateful to Terry Russell for the car drawing. Tickets are from Godfrey Croughton's collection. Timetables and maps are produced by kind permission of the London Trandsport Museum.

Readers will note that there is an overlap in coverage with companion volume *Kingston and Wimbledon Tramways*. I have tried wherever possible not to duplicate views.

GEOGRAPHICAL SETTING

Twickenham and the area adjacent to Hampton Court on the north bank of the Thames were once situated in the County of Middlesex. The south bank of the Thames lay in the County of Surrey. In 1965 the advent of Greater London changed many local boundaries and large London Boroughs took over many of the functions of the previous county councils, but Surrey County Hall remained at Kingston. A large oasis of green in this otherwise urban area is formed by Bushy Park, once a royal hunting ground. The electric tram route circumnavigated it.

HISTORICAL BACKGROUND

There were no horse tramways in the area, and those people who could not afford train fares would normally have had to walk. This situation was changed by Sir James Clifton Robinson and his London United Tramways Company. Robinson was in many respects the I.K.Brunel of the tramway world - he would very rarely take "no" for an answer. He was a fervent supporter of cheap and reliable public transport. These noble aims are just as valid at the end of the twentieth century as they were in the last decade of the nineteenth.

Inspite of opposition from the "establishment" and vested interests like the London &

South Western Railway Company, construction pushed ahead from the two London termini of Hammersmith and Shepherds Bush. A branch from the Hammersmith to Hounslow trunk tramway at Busch Corner opened to traffic on 13th August 1902. It was extended from Coles Bridge to Cross Deep, Twickenham on 13th September 1902. A planned "by-pass" tram route to Kew Bridge was begun with the opening on 13th September 1902 of the section between King Street, Twickenham and a terminal in St.Margaret's Road on the approach to Richmond Bridge. Unfortunately this grand scheme of constructing an alternative route to London came to nought, as the LUT were never able to electrify the Kew to Richmond horse tramway. (This track is fully described in *Hammersmith and Hounslow Tramways*).

On 8th November 1902 trams reached Stanley Road junction, Fulwell, and the completion of the "Hampton Loop" occurred on 2nd April 1903 when electric trams started to serve Hampton Court, Hampton Wick and Hampton Hill. The system then settled down until the next bout of construction in 1905-06. On 1st March 1906 lines opened across Kingston Bridge to Thames Ditton, Kingston Hill and Tolworth. Local routes from Kingston to Ham Boundary, and from the town to Richmond Park Gates came into service on 26th May 1906. On the same day electric trams were extended from Norbiton Church to Malden Fountain. The link to Wimbledon was opened in two stages: Malden Fountain to Raynes Park on 27th April 1907, and Raynes Park to Wimbledon on 2nd May 1907.

Services were generally worked by open top cars and the new type T "Palace" cars which represented the height of contemporary luxury. Sadly for the inhabitants of Kingston these fine

ROBERT J. HARLEY FEBRUARY 1999.

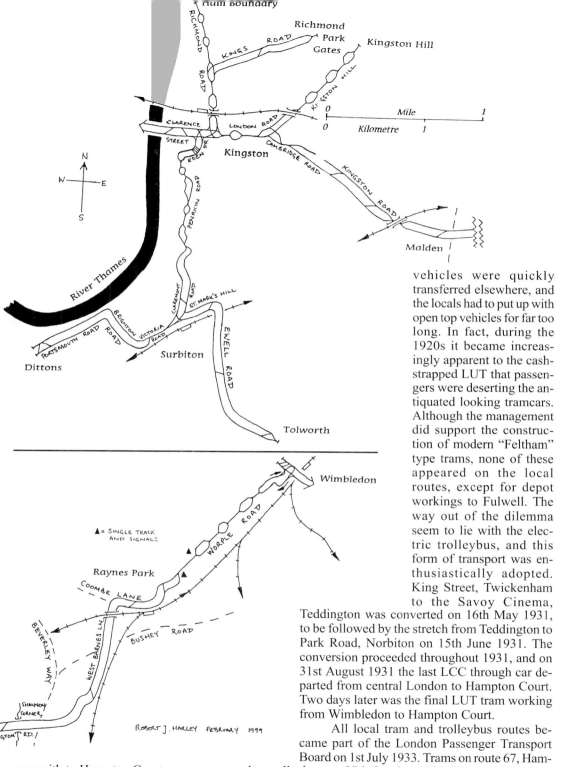

Ham Boundary

Richmond Park Gates

Kingston Hill

RICHMOND ROAD

KINGS ROAD

KINGSTON HILL

Mile

Kilometre

CLARENCE STREET

LONDON ROAD

EDEN SR

Kingston

CAMBRIDGE ROAD

KINGSTON ROAD

N
W — E
S

River Thames

PENRHYN ROAD

CLAREMONT ROAD

ST. MARK'S HILL

BRIGHTON ROAD

VICTORIA ROAD

EWELL ROAD

PORTSMOUTH ROAD

Dittons

Surbiton

Tolworth

Malden

Wimbledon

▲ = SINGLE TRACK AND SIGNALS

WORPLE ROAD

Raynes Park

COOMBE LANE

BEVERLEY WAY

WEST BARNES LN

BUSHEY ROAD

SHANNON CORNER

KINGTON RD.

ROBERT J. HARLEY FEBRUARY 1999

vehicles were quickly transferred elsewhere, and the locals had to put up with open top vehicles for far too long. In fact, during the 1920s it became increasingly apparent to the cash-strapped LUT that passengers were deserting the antiquated looking tramcars. Although the management did support the construction of modern "Feltham" type trams, none of these appeared on the local routes, except for depot workings to Fulwell. The way out of the dilemma seem to lie with the electric trolleybus, and this form of transport was enthusiastically adopted. King Street, Twickenham to the Savoy Cinema, Teddington was converted on 16th May 1931, to be followed by the stretch from Teddington to Park Road, Norbiton on 15th June 1931. The conversion proceeded throughout 1931, and on 31st August 1931 the last LCC through car departed from central London to Hampton Court. Two days later was the final LUT tram working from Wimbledon to Hampton Court.

All local tram and trolleybus routes became part of the London Passenger Transport Board on 1st July 1933. Trams on route 67, Hammersmith to Hampton Court, were converted to trolleybus on 27th October 1935. Thus ended the era of railbound street transport.

RICHMOND BRIDGE BRANCH

1. A more accurate description of the location of the terminus could be East Twickenham. Whatever the semantics, car 212 stands at the end of the track opposite Morley Road. The Richmond Bridge to Hampton Court (via Hampton Wick) service was inaugurated in April 1903; after several changes it settled down as service 69 with a southern terminal at Kingston, Eden Street.

3. Car 296 takes the curve by the Rising Sun, at St.Margaret's, Twickenham. The nearby St.Margaret's Station (featured in the Middleton Press, *Waterloo to Windsor* album) was little affected by the advent of the tramway.

2. Car 179 stands at the terminus with Richmond Bridge in the distance. This was a very unsatisfactory situation, as the rails were never extended to reach Richmond, Barnes or Putney. Thus a valuable link in the London tramway network was never forged. Eventually the Richmond Bridge branch withered on the vine and it was replaced by buses on 1st October 1924.

4. Note the informative stop sign on the right of this picture of car 89 in York Street. Ahead of the tram is a crossover which enabled short working cars to reverse without hampering traffic movements in King Street. Car 89 belonged to type Z and entered service in a rich Venetian red and white livery.

6. We remain in York Street, from which car 287 is just emerging. This postcard view poses something of a puzzle in that the fashions and the point controller suggest a date around 1908. A commercial purpose seems to be behind the adding of "Kingsway Buildings 1926 Twickenham". Was this photo used in support of a 1920s campaign to update the image of Twickenham?

5. Car 286 is seen at the west end of York Street. The date must be close to the September 1902 opening of this branch. A four wheel "Growler" cab waits for shoppers who chose not to avail themselves of the penny tramfares.

TWICKENHAM

7.   We are looking at an essential task of tramway operation - permanent way maintenance. Here by Mogden Lane, Twickenham new rails are being lowered into position. LUT car 290 waits for the PW Department lorry to move out of the way. Even after tramway abandonment much of the track in London Road remained in situ, and ironically it outlived the replacing trolleybuses.

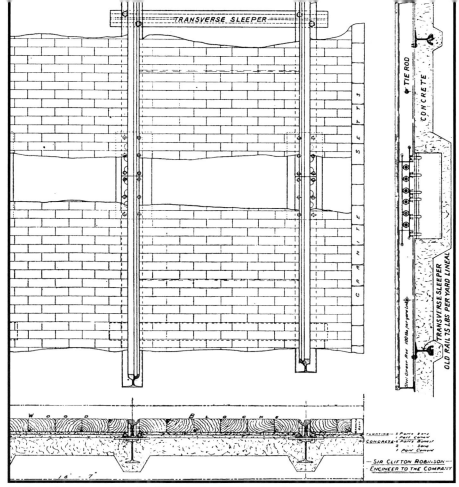

Rails and track used by the LUT in the 1906 extensions.

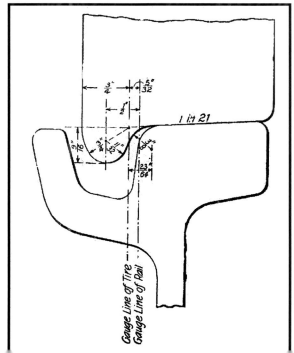

8.   In King Street, Twickenham looking south west from Church Street we view car 248 with its indicator blind set to HAMMERSMITH DISTRICT RAILWAY. Boards on the side of the tram give a more traditional itinerary of intermediate towns on the route. Car 248 belongs to type W and is painted in royal blue and white.

9.   Opposite the King's Head Hotel car 183 sets off for Hampton Court, whilst in the foreground a sister vehicle edges out of York Street. It is on the Richmond Bridge to Hampton Court via Hampton Hill service. Note the LUT inspector standing on the traffic island to the right of the picture.

10.   In the other direction to the previous view, we are now looking from King Street at cars 288 and 270.

11. In 1931 a trolleybus turning circle was constructed here. No doubt the photographer wished to emphasise the difference between the old, open top tramcar and the new, all enclosed trolleybus. From the look of the bunting on HX 3983 it may well be opening day, 16th May 1931.

12.   Car 300 traverses the single track section in King Street.

13.   Electric trams first reached this location, King Street by Cross Deep, on 13th September 1902. Lines from here to Stanley Road junction were put into commission on 8th November 1902. Car 174 is spotted with a full load of excursionists, shortly after the opening of the full service to Hampton Court on 2nd April 1903.

→

15. Later in the 1920s vehicular traffic became more of a problem for the trams. The conductor of car 210 puts out his arm to warn the oncoming lorry that passengers are crossing the road from the pavement to board his tramcar. The route number 67 was allocated in 1912 to the Hammersmith - Hampton Court service. The journey time was just over the hour and the through fare was a mere sixpence (2.5p)!

14. The tree lined Heath Road is the setting for cars 223 and 159.

→

16. Holy Trinity Church looks out over car 270 and Twickenham Green. This postcard view is franked 4th October 1904. On the back the sender has written "the place is so altered and built up that one would not know it". No doubt the trams contributed to this building boom.

17. Car 193 on service 69 passes Holy Trinity Church, Twickenham. The building dates from 1839-41 and is a classic example of the Victorian Gothic Revival style.

Route map of the LUT system immediately prior to the first trolleybus conversions. The dotted lines indicate LCC connecting tramways.

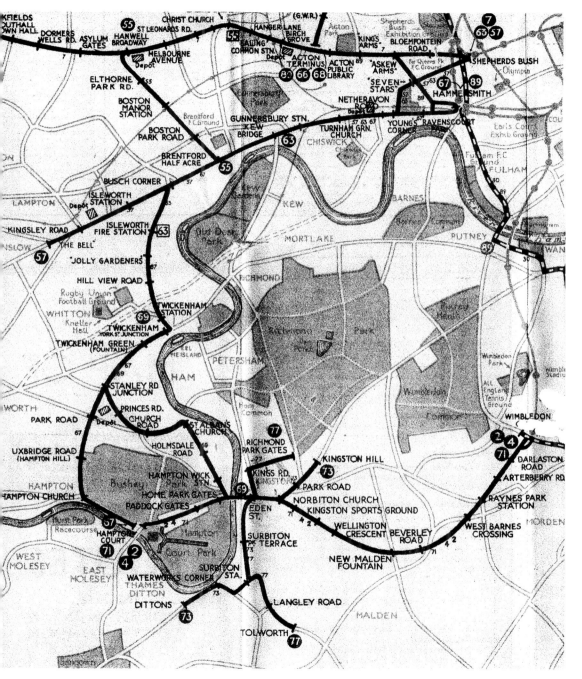

18. Hampton Road, Twickenham by the junction of Third Cross Road is the location for this view which is dated circa 1909. Car 200 has left in its wake a rather bemused policeman who regards the photographer with a "what 'ave we 'ere" look!

19. Where Hampton Road joins Stanley Road, the tramway lines diverged, leading to Hampton Court and Teddington respectively. On the right, a northbound car waits for car 272 to clear the junction.

20. We now look in a the opposite direction to the previous view. Car 246 takes centre stage, whilst on the extreme left, an LUT pointsman waits for the next southbound tramcar. This official became redundant in 1909 when Turner automatic point controllers were installed at this junction. At night if the points were set for Stanley Road, a green aspect would feature on the lamp positioned above the point lever box. A white light indicated a clear road straight ahead.

21. One final look at Stanley Road junction reveals cars 274 and 220, with an inspector standing in the middle of the road between them. In recent years this entrance to Stanley Road has been blocked off, and traffic now roars along and pollutes the A311 Hampton Road. The environmentally friendly qualities of the trams and trolleybuses are but a cherished memory.

22. Many years have now passed and we are now at the end of the trolleybus era in 1962. The Nelson Inn still occupies its place at the Corner of Stanley Road and Hampton Road. Hampton Court to Hammersmith tram route 67 gave way to trolleybus route 667 which in turn was ousted by diesel bus route 267.

FULWELL DEPOT

23. George Gundry was on hand to record the movements of car 341 as it left Fulwell Depot one day in 1922. This experimental vehicle is fully described in companion volume *Kingston and Wimbledon Tramways*.

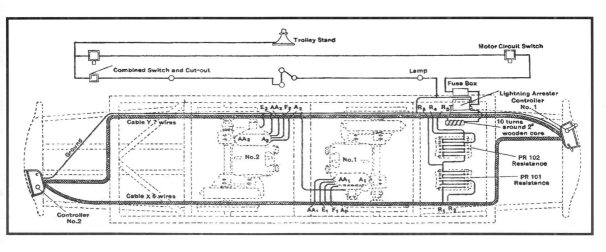

24. The next large experiment conducted by the LUT was the introduction of trolleybuses in place of tramcars. Here outside Fulwell Depot car 296 meets its nemesis. This early LUT trolleybus network later formed the basis of the enormous LT system which was once the largest in the world.

25. This type T car is now in London Transport livery as it passes the entrance gates to the depot in Wellington Road.

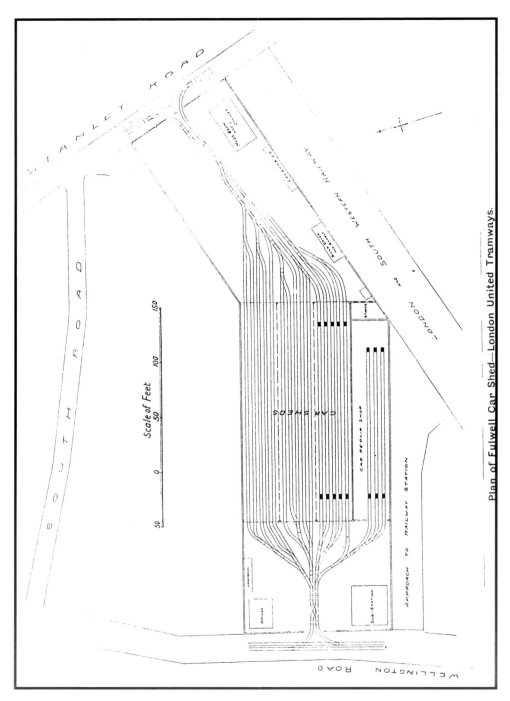

Plan of Fulwell Car Shed—London United Tramways.

Plan of Fulwell Car Sheds

26. The point iron is used to switch tracks for car 18, now well past its prime and facing an early demise under the new trolleybus regime. Part of the large Fulwell Depot forms the backdrop to this scene. In the foreground can be seen a single tongued point and trackwork in somewhat parlous condition. Many of these rails lasted for decades as a mute witness to a past age.

27. Fulwell Depot was laid out on an 11 acre/ 4.4 ha site and it was envisaged that it would hold 100 trams. As it turned out, the depot was more than able to accommodate the local LUT fleet. This evening scene from 1931 depicts a new Feltham type car which contrasts favourably with the antique appearance of its sister vehicles.

28. One corner of the depot forecourt was referred to as the "boneyard", and in the years 1930/31 it witnessed the destruction of many members of the LUT fleet. Here cars 341, 30 and 344 meet their end.

29. On the east side of the depot, looking from Stanley Road, we are treated to the spectacle of "all systems go" for the new trolleybus service. From 1931 the trams were restricted to only five roads in the depot.

TEDDINGTON

30. Broad Street, Teddington and car 99 rumbles past the fruiterers on the corner. The driver of the open tourer MF 1934 will attest to the fact that parking was no problem in those days. Note that the traction standards on the left side of the road also carried the company's telephone link from Kingston to Fulwell Depot.

31. The Old Parish Church is the setting for car 300 which has the road to itself. On the right next to the smart chap in the boater is a fire alarm pillar; the neighbouring gas lamp is marked with the legend FIRE ALARM on the glass just above the burner.

32. Car 283 in High Street, Teddington was obviously considered a suitable subject for a Christmas card. The locals were probably quite proud of their new trams and wished to show them off to the rest of the world. In April 1903 when the electric trams first arrived here, much of London, then the greatest city in the world, was still stuck in the horse drawn era.

HAMPTON WICK

33. The railway bridge carrying the tracks to Hampton Wick Station lies to the rear of car 290. The tram is about to pull up at the stop by the trailing crossover in High Street, Hampton Wick. This station and others in the area are featured in *Kingston and Hounslow Loops*.

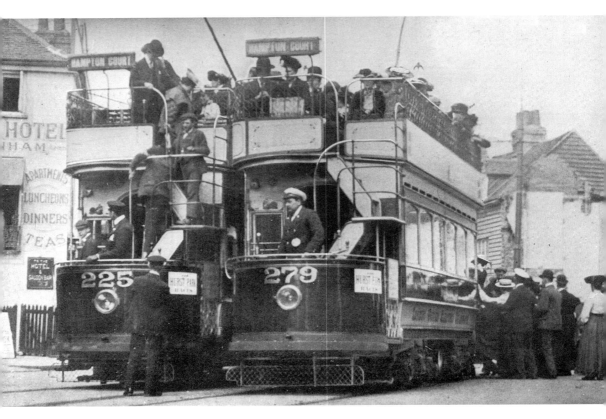

34. Cars 225 and 279 seem to be working "specials" in connection with Hurst Park races. One wonders whether the throng consists of folk who have walked across Kingston Bridge for the tram connection to Hampton Court.

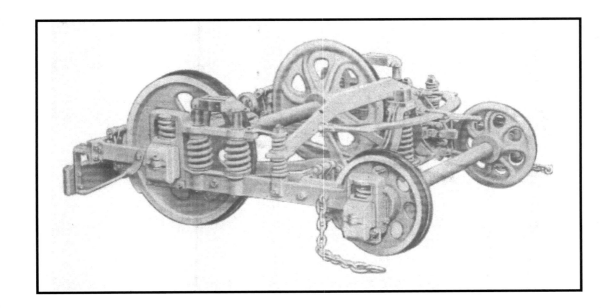

35. This is a 1906 view of car 309 at Hampton Wick High Street. This vehicle is probably working the shortlived Dittons (Windows Bridge) to Richmond Bridge service. These type T cars only lasted a few months in the Kingston area and in the spring of 1907 they were moved to other parts of the LUT.

36. We look north from Old Bridge Street and the approach to Kingston Bridge. Lower Teddington Road forks right in the distance. Car 189 is the only mechanised transport about, thus it is perfectly safe for the cyclist to ride on the wrong side of the road.

37. The White Hart Hotel overlooks the triangular junction of lines leading to Kingston, Hampton Court and Teddington. Car 70 is about to swing to the motorman's left so as to gain the tracks over Kingston Bridge. The centre island with the tram stop sign was a marvellous place to stand just to watch the trams go by, and as such, was a favourite location of LUT inspectors!

38. Although the points have been laid, there are as yet no connecting rails over Kingston Bridge. This dates the scene to 1903-06. Car 211 is about to pull away in the direction of Hampton Court. The bridge was almost doubled in width in 1914.

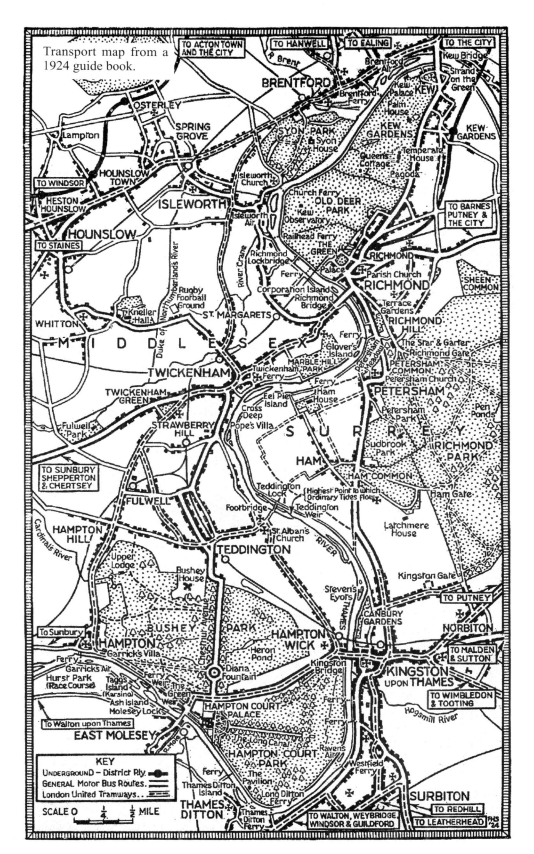

Transport map from a 1924 guide book.

39. About three years later than the previous card and the trams seem to be well established on their new routes. On the left is an open top type W car, and on the bridge over the Thames is a type T which is possibly working the Kingston Hill to Hampton Court line.

───────────▶

41. Car 308 has just left Bridge Foot, Hampton Wick and the motorman is applying more power to the motors as he gains speed along Hampton Court Road. This stretch was one of the fastest on any London tramway, and there was little intermediate traffic to halt progress until Hampton Court terminus was reached.

40. One can assume that this picture was taken roughly the same time as the previous one. An inspector checks something with the motorman of car 303, whilst car 292 gets ready to "bag" the right of way along Hampton Court Road. This would have been a colourful scene with the green of the trees contrasting with the royal blue and white livery of car 292 and the Venetian red and white paint scheme of car 303.

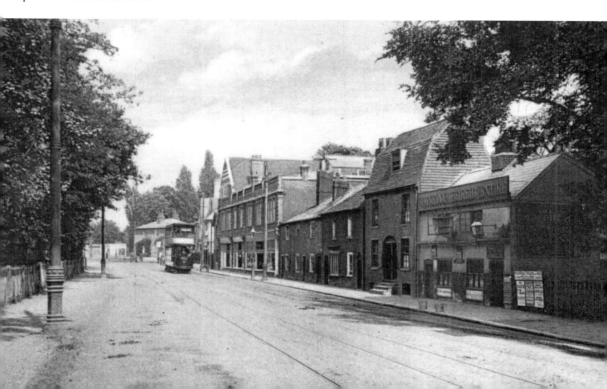

HAMPTON COURT

42. The area round Hampton Court is steeped in history. Hampton Court Palace, the famous maze and the adjoining grounds generated substantial excursion revenue for the LUT. The old narrow bridge across the Thames was reconstructed in 1931 about 25 years after this view was taken. Car 230 is en route to Richmond Bridge, and across the way passengers are boarding a tram for the reurn trip to London via Twickenham, Brentford and Chiswick.

44. Car 287 stands at what should have been the start of a further tramway extension over the bridge and on to Thames Ditton where a connection would have been made with one of the Kingston local routes. Unfortunately the lines stayed firmly on the drawing board.

43. A very similar scene at Hampton Court terminus, only this time the weather isn't so inviting. No doubt the Bank Holiday crowds who benefitted from a 24 mile round trip from Hammersmith, and paid a mere shilling (5p) for the priviledge, would soon be back. As one contemporary guide remarked, this journey was a better "bob's worth" than anything else offered in the capital.

45. We are now looking from the bridge approach and on an island we observe the conductor of car 219 as he attends to the trolley rope. This was normally wound round the trolley pole so that it did not get in the way of top deck passengers. By contrast on the Shepherds Bush bound car the rope is being used to swing the trolley ready for the return journey.

46. The gates to Hampton Court Palace add a suitably regal touch to the background as car 289 waits at the terminus. The sign on the traction standard points visitors to Hampton Court Station, which was situated on the Surrey side of the Thames: see *Branch Lines around Effingham Junction*.

47. Trippers pack car 250 as it prepares to leave. An LUT inspector looks past the photographer; no doubt, there is yet another tram waiting to use the terminal stub.

48. LT car 2364, formerly LUT car 212 of type U, catches the sunshine of a late summer's day in 1934. Service 67 has only a few months left to run before the overhead wire crews arrive to install all the new trolleybus equipment. The car itself was scrapped in July 1936. This tram can be seen in original condition in picture 22. Behind the white rail is Hampton Court Green, the site of regular crowd drawing amusement fairs.

49. Caught on film about the same time as the previous view, car 2360 (ex-LUT car 158) is empty, having just arrived. Part of the Palace is in the background.

50. LUT car 247 was a "one off" vehicle of type XU. Logically it had a type X lower deck which was married to a type U top deck, hence the new classification. Here it is masquerading as LT car 2411. Note the remnants of the eastbound curves to the former route from Hampton Court to Kingston. By the time this photo was taken, trolleybuses had supplanted trams and passengers desirous of reaching Kingston or Wimbledon had to use railless traction. When trams to Hammersmith were abandoned, a roundabout was constructed and used by all trolleybuses as a turning circle.

51. We head for Hampton and as we walk along Hampton Court Road we pass car 2373 outside the Cardinal Wolsey. Beyond this spot is Tagg's Island, which was the location of Fred Karno's Karsino, an amusement palace for whose patrons the LUT laid on late night trams. These would reverse at a crossover situated some yards behind the tram in this picture. The Green is on the right.

52. Garrick's Villa takes its name from the famous actor, David Garrick (1716-1779), who laid out the estate in the 1750s. The property was purchased by the LUT in 1902 and a siding was added to accommodate excursion trams. These were used in connection with staff social events hosted by Sir James and Lady Robinson. In this 1957 view, taken by John Gillham, we see the site of the tramway siding next to the corner of Church Street, Hampton. Garrick's Villa was put up for sale in 1910 and the siding was lifted shortly afterwards.

53. Car 185 is at Pantile Bridge over the River Longford which was an artificial channel excavated to supply water to Hampton Court. It is seen from the junction with Uxbridge Road, with the Congregational Church in the background.

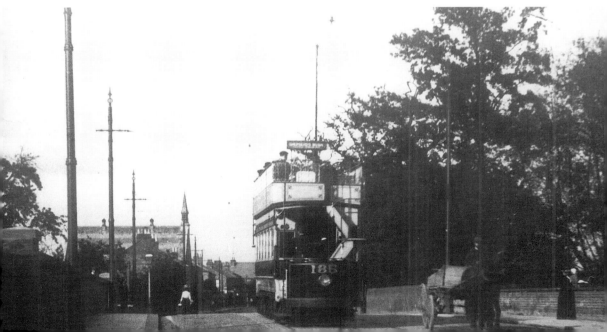

HAMPTON HILL

54. Some parts of Hampton Hill High Street received single track before the LUT was able to obtain permission to widen the carriageway. Car 255 negotiates a potential bottleneck outside the post office. By 1909 all the single track and passing loop sections in the area had been replaced by double track.

55. Car 177 is bound for Hampton Court and has just passed over the now busy crossroads, which was supplied with traffic lights in the 1930s. Park Road is on the right. To the east of Hampton lies Bushy Park and the LUT had to get special permission from the Crown to take thin strips of the royal freehold so that road widening could take place. Fortunately King Edward VII and Sir James Clifton Robinson seem to have got on quite well!

KINGSTON

56. Pomp and ceremony at Kingston as the Mayor pilots car 320 in the inaugural run on 1st March 1906. Note the splendid uniforms of the LUT staff with their white topped caps.

57. Clarence Street, Kingston is the setting for car 171 which is en route for Tooting. Here connection would be made for London County Council trams to central London. The Hampton Court to Tooting service opened on 27th June 1907.

58. Tracks curve in front of the photographer into Eden Street. The other lines are in Clarence Street. Car 332 is probably working the Tolworth to Richmond Park Gates service.

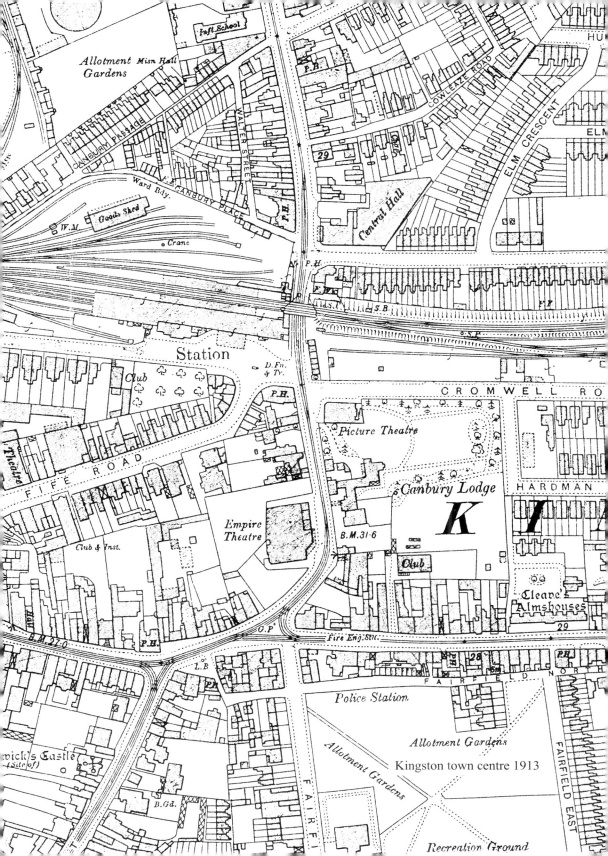

Kingston town centre 1913

569 KINGSTON ON-THAMES.
Clarence Street. — LL

59. We look in the other direction to the previous view. The type T cars have now left the area and open top trams like car 277 now rule the roost. Richmond Road is to the right foreground, whilst London Road diverges to the left. In the distance is the junction of Eden Street and Clarence Street. The lone motor vehicle is a portent of things to come!

60. Car 238 is in Eden Street and is about to turn into St.James's Road. On the traction standard above the sign for Surbiton is a 10 mph speed limit warning. One wonders whether the town planners in 1910 could have envisaged a situation where traffic congestion would have forced the pedestrianisation of many streets in central Kingston. At the close of the twentieth century any driver in an urban area would be very lucky to average ten miles an hour!

SURBITON

61. Trams were (and are) a very reliable form of transport. Thus a fall of snow was all in a day's work for the hardy souls of the London United Tramways. Their motto was "the service must go on", and go on it did, with the help of muscle power in clearing tracks and junctions. Here in Claremont Road, Surbiton the local inhabitants must be relieved that they can depend on their transport system.

62. Car 277 reappears, this time under the watchful eye of an LUT inspector, who has selected the optimum location to observe passing tramcars.

63. The stop signs on the right hand side of Claremont Road indicate the two destinations of Tolworth and Windows Bridge to the prospective traveller. Of course there was always a conductor on the tram to provide further assistance if need be - all of which is a far cry from the "one person operated" public transport of recent times.

64. Here we look north along Claremont Road, with St.Mark's Hill on the right, and Surbiton Station behind the camera. This station is featured in the *Waterloo to Woking* album.

65. M.Griggs, Drapers, on the corner of Victoria Road and Claremont Road, was a frequent advertiser on the tramcars. No doubt this helped to bring customers to the front door on their shopping expeditions. For many folk the advent of cheap and reliable trams enabled them to partake of a freedom of movement, and of choice, unobtainable in the days when suburban railways had the monopoly. The LUT syphoned much traffic away from the steam hauled lines of the LSWR.

LONG DITTON

66. In a westerly direction from Victoria Road lay Long Ditton tram terminus, right outside the post office. The crew of car 299 take a break from their duties to have their image preserved for posterity.

67. The Windows Bridge, Long Ditton to Kingston Hill service later received the number 73. Here the conductor of car 174 seems to be adjusting his cap before the onslaught of a party determined to benefit from the open air charms of the top deck. We are looking north-east along Portsmouth Road.

68. Time moves on to the late 1920s and car 152 waits for departure on a short working to Kingston, Eden Street. At least the upper deck passengers are now shielded from the elements, but they still have to run the gauntlet of open staircases. To the left of the tram is a fire alarm pillar - penalty for improper use £20! Along the street another tram waits to enter the terminus; the service interval was a car every ten minutes.

TOLWORTH

69. On the south-east side of Surbiton lies Tolworth, where the tracks ended just opposite the Red Lion. Tramway operation here lasted from 1906 to July 1931 when trolleybuses were instituted. The motorman of car 258 looks thoroughly miserable, in tune with the winter weather.

70. This is a fine three quarter shot of car 258, which was taken on the same day as the previous view. The road partly obscured by the tram was later wired for a turning loop used by LT trolleybus route 603, and as such retained electric traction until the end of trolleybuses in London in May 1962.

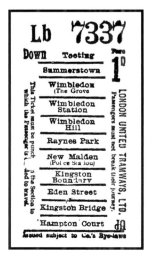

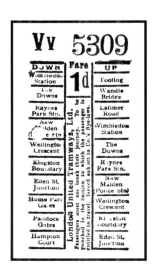

71. At Kingston Hill a member of type W stands broadside to the camera. One wonders why the LUT persisted in running so many open top cars when they presented such an antiquated image to the fare paying public. Certainly the weak state of the LUT's finances had a lot to do with the decision to use these cars until they wore out.

72. One LUT modernisation project that did get the go ahead was the alteration of car 341 to one man operation. The experiment was never particularly successful and the vehicle is seen here at Richmond Park Gates whilst working route 77 to Tolworth.

73. We continue to follow the fortunes of car 258, observed here at Richmond Park Gates terminus. From this angle it certainly seems that anno domini has been playing havock with the bodywork - the is a distinct "droop" noticeable in the platforms and ends of the lower saloon. Aside from this, the general condition and paintwork of the tram are more than satisfactory.

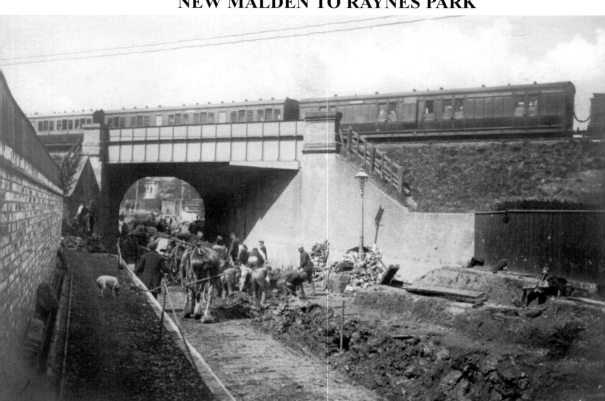

74.   One of the LUT's greatest assets was its loyal workforce and this "pick and shovel" work illustrates some of the feverish activity encountered at the railway bridge on Kingston Road. The road level under the bridge will also need to be lowered to permit the passage of double deck tramcars. Provided the weather holds, the track gangs will pass this way shortly and the first rails will be laid. After them the overhead wire team will commence installing standards and erecting the direct current traction wires.

Kingston Road railway bridge 1913

75.   Work has now been completed and car 295 creeps gingerly under the bridge. Restricted clearances have necessitated the use of single track at this location. The brick arch originally carried the London and Southampton Railway.

76. In this 1920s view streetlamps and pavements have been added to the layout. Car 18 on service 71 poses with an inspector. The steel spans were added by the LSWR during quadrupling of the main line railway.

77. On the Kingston side of the bridge we see the same inspector as appeared in the previous shot. This time he accompanies car 78 which is working to Hampton Court. Note that these top covered trams only just squeezed under the bridge and the trolley pole was forced down almost to the roof as it kept contact with the overhead wire.

78. Life proceeds at a comfortable pace in Kingston Road, New Malden. The sounds of the lone cyclist and the bright blue and white tramcar barely impinge on the tranquillity of the scene.

79. We are not told whether Mr Deacon, landlord of the Duke of Wellington, was present at the opening celebrations, but here on 23rd May 1906, the Board of Trade inspectors may well have wanted to talk to him about the position of his inn sign. Of course the removal expenses would have been down to the LUT. Public service started three days later.

80. Cars 142 and 141 are depicted "on ferry duty" at Shannon Corner, Burlington Road where Beverley Brook is traversed by the highway. Normal service cars would have waited at a safe distance from the inundation and passengers would have been shuttled on these specially adapted, coupled cars. This is indicative of the tramway company's commitment to getting its passengers through, come what may.

81. On Coombe Lane, Raynes Park by the corner of Durham Road we encounter car 287. The rural surroundings are typical of the nature of this tram route before the interwar house building spree.

Raynes Park is shown on the 1913 edition. The railway junction is illustrated in the *Wimbledon to Epsom* album. North is to the left of the page.

82. There were no patrol cars in those days and the bobby on the bike constituted the mobile presence of the local constabulary. Notice that here is another example of a cyclist keeping between the tramlines, rather than riding on the crudely laid macadam between the wood block setts and the kerb. Car 217 is about to pass the Raynes Park Hotel.

WIMBLEDON

83. Nearing the end of our journey we traverse Worple Road, Wimbledon. Car 279 waits at a loop for a car coming in the opposite direction to clear the single track. This area is also featured in companion album, *Kingston and Wimbledon Tramways*.

84. We leave the LUT at Wimbledon Broadway with this view looking past the Town Hall at the junction of Queen's Road. We also leave behind an unhurried era where cheap, reliable and pollution free tramway travel broadened the horizons of so many Londoners.

ROLLING STOCK

Type Z cars 1-100 were built in 1901 by Hurst, Nelson of Motherwell, they rode on Peckham 14D2 maximum traction trucks. Sixty-six trams of this type were top covered in 1910-11 and were reclassified type Y.

85. Motorman and conductor are at their stations in this fine broadside view of a type Z car. Each vehicle seated 30 in the lower saloon and 39 on the upper deck. The original livery was Venetian red and white; trucks were painted in red oxide.

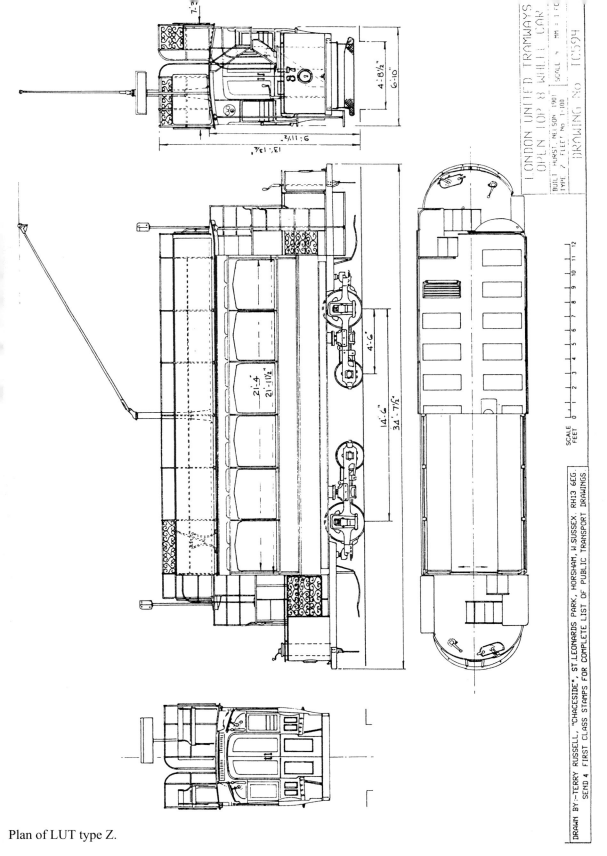

LONDON UNITED TRAMWAYS
OPEN TOP 8 WHEEL CAR
BUILT HURST, NELSON 1901 | SCALE 4 MM = 1 FO
TYPE Z FLEET No 1-100   DRAWING No TC3594

SCALE 0 1 2 3 4 5 6 7 8 9 10 11 12
FEET

4'-8½"
6'-10"
5'-11½"
13'-13¾"

21'-4'
21'-11½'
4'-6'
14'-6'
34'-7½'

DRAWN BY:- TERRY RUSSELL, "CHACESIDE", ST.LEONARDS PARK, HORSHAM, W.SUSSEX. RH13 6EG.
SEND 4 FIRST CLASS STAMPS FOR COMPLETE LIST OF PUBLIC TRANSPORT DRAWINGS.

Plan of LUT type Z.

86. In 1909 car 52 was experimentally eqipped with a Barber six wheel truck. It had a few trips up and down Uxbridge Road before the test was terminated and the normal bogies were restored.

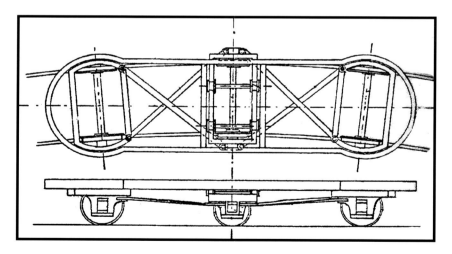

Sketch plan of the Barber six wheel truck as used experimentally under car 52. The principle was that the axles would turn slightly so that they were in line with the radius of the curve. The Cleminson system had the same objective and is described in *Branch Line to Southwold*.

87. After a few years the design of trams like car 89 began to look very antiquated. No top deck cover and no protection whatsoever for the hardy motorman was not a satisfactory situation. In winter this must have been a truly unpleasant experience. Note that advertisements have now appeared on the car.

88. Car 1 is depicted towards the end of its working life. The top deck cover still looks as if it has been added as an afterthought, and the different size upper and lower saloon windows do not enhance its aesthetic appeal. In fact the whole shape is downright ungainly. The bulk of these cars were scrapped when the lines they served were replaced by LUT trolleybuses.

90. In 1911 car 175 was converted to a single deck "luxury" car which was to cater for the private hire market. The interior fittings were all sumptous and there was a space for a buffet at one end of the car. In 1924 this vehicle together with cars 178 and 275 was further rebuilt into a type S2 vestibuled one man operated tram (fleet nos. 342-344; illustrated in *Shepherds Bush and Uxbridge Tramways*). It was withdrawn in 1928.

89. Type Y, formerly type Z, has slightly more style when viewed from this angle. However, we know from passenger reports that the top decks were cold and draughty and that the protruding trolley standard allowed the ingress of rainwater. All in all, it is no wonder that the replacing trolleybuses were welcomed with open arms.

LONDON
UNITED TRAMWAYS

SPECIAL SALOON CAR

FOR HIRE FOR THEATRE, CONCERT, BALL PARTIES, Etc.
WEDDINGS AND OTHER SOCIAL EVENTS

RATE:—7/6 RETURN FOR EACH PENNY OF THE ORDINARY SINGLE FARE.

EXAMPLE OF CHARGES
TWICKENHAM TO HAMMERSMITH
SINGLE FARE BY TRAM, 4d.
CHARGE FOR CAR AND 20 PASSENGERS
OR UNDER £1.10-0

FULL PARTICULARS FROM
LONDON UNITED TRAMWAY Co.,
74, HIGH ROAD, CHISWICK.

91. This LUT poster was used to advertise car 175. One wonders whether this was the nearest London got to a true Pullman style tram service!

→

92. Appropriately we begin with LUT staff. Crew members are pictured here are in their summer uniforms which featured white topped caps. Each driver and conductor worked two shifts per car which amounted to around ten hours a day.

→

93. By the end of the LUT era the uniform hadn't changed much. Note the conductor with his leather cash bag; he is performing one of his traditional duties, that of turning the trolley. The motorman has just removed the key from the front controller and he is about to walk through the lower saloon to activate the controller at the other end - such was the simplicity of operating a double ended vehicle.

STAFF UNIFORMS

94. Inspite of being employed by London Transport, these two still retain the old South Metropolitan uniforms. White cap tops were worn each year from 1st May to 1st October. The material was blue serge with red piping.

95. The London County Council went in for navy blue serge with double breasted greatcoats for motormen, as illustrated here. Women conductors, employed during the First World War, were issued with a navy blue linen skirt, a jacket with patch pockets and a panama style hat.

96. Motormen needed to be muffled up to cope with standing on open platforms in inclement weather. It was only in the 1930s that driver's vestibules came into greater use on London's trams. The conductor has his cash bag, ticket punch and his whistle.

97. Some Croydon Corporation employees affected a rather dapper style, perhaps they felt a certain "municipal pride" in their jobs. One suspects that the motorman pictured here regularly polished his coat buttons and his cap badge. It would be unfair to compare him with the sloppy turn out which passes as uniform for some modern day bus drivers!

98. Erith Urban District Council started with an attractive fleet of apple green painted tramcars. Staff on the new venture were kitted out in the standard navy blue. The conductor has his Williamson ticket punch and the motorman has removed his goggles for the photographer.

99. This 1952 shot by John Meredith, shows the last uniform worn by London tramway staff. The original LT outfit of navy blue serge with red piping on the trouser seams, jacket lapels and on the cap top had been replaced by more utility materials. This was as a result of wartime shortages. Only blue piping was retained on the trouser seams. Note the conductor has now discarded his cap, but the motorman and the two inspectors wear the normal red "bullseye and bar" LT cap badges.

100. On the last day, 5th July 1952, these four are about to trade in their "T" Metropolitan Stage Carriage badges for the "N" central bus ones. The crew on the left are sporting the lightweight summer jackets. Smartness was still the order of the day.

101. Depot workers and repair men wore leather aprons or old suits before their employers got round to supply good quality overalls. Early tramcar maintenace was labour intensive as this view inside a Croydon depot illustrates. Woe betide anyone who mislaid any of the tools!

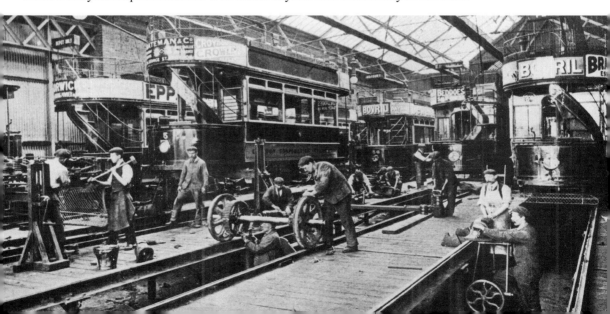

102. Oilskins and sou'westers gave the cleaning staff a somewhat nautical appearance. In those days the idea of sending a tram out on the road in a dirty condition was anathema to depot staff. They took a pride in their work at Holloway Depot.

103. By the early 1930s employers tended to be less autocratic and staff had more benefits. This relaxed group at Charlton Works stand in front of their "baby", the new LCC car 1. Overalls have now been provided, but even so most working men still wore a tie and cleaned their shoes regularly. This was still a world away from the jeans, T shirt and trainers culture.

ACCIDENTS

104. Provided track and cars are well maintained, tramway travel is one of the safest forms of transport. However, even in the best regulated families accidents happen, as here where an "I" section girder seems to have bisected the top deck of car 89. As is usual in any sort of tramway contretemps, a large crowd of spectators has gathered. The staff of the horse drawn tower waggon will have their work cut out to clear the tracks and restore normal service.

105. The date is 8th June 1911 and car 268 has probably been engaged in a right of way dispute with a brewer's dray. Kingston Road, New Malden is effectively blocked as police and LUT inspectors try to remedy the situation.

106. On Easter Monday, 1st April 1907, SMET car 19 lost braking power in Park Lane, Wallington, picked up speed and overturned on the corner of Ruskin Road. Two people were killed and thirty injured. At the subsequent enquiry the motorman was blamed for his inexperience.

107. Most damaged cars were towed back to the depot, there to await the arrival of insurance assessors. Finally the vehicle would receive the expert attention of the resident coachbuilders. Generally, trams were very well built and the other road vehicle in the collision usually came off worse.

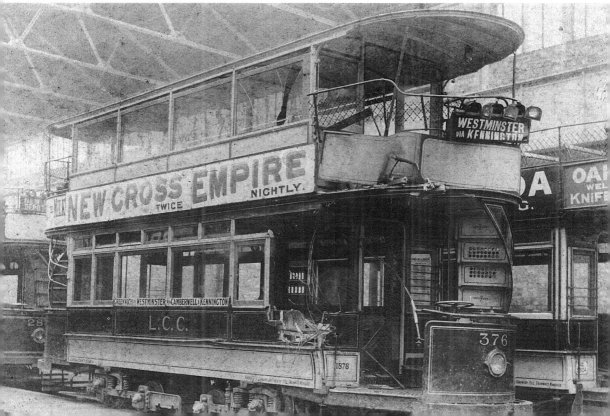

108. Sensationalism is no new journalistic phenomenon, witness here on 2nd September 1911, at Shardeloes Road junction, Brockley, when postcards were produced for the "LCC Tram Disaster". Car 110 derailed on the slope of Shardeloes Road and overturned in Lewisham High Road. Forty-two passengers were on board and there was one fatality.

110. In May 1933, LCC car 1564 left the track at Herne Hill and headed into the nearest United Dairies shop. In the previous month the Ministry of Transport had given permission for a rise in the speed limit governing LCC trams. On this occasion one is left to speculate whether this was a totally wise decision.

109. Car 150 has slewed across Lee High Road, just short of Lee Green terminus. Behind the stricken tram is the old Lee Green picture palace, later known as the Savoy Cinema.

111. Almost no words are necessary - this photo taken in the mid-1930s says it all. Car 1545 is guided gently back towards the depot, with an LT breakdown vehicle supplying the motive power. The tram was reconditioned by London Transport and lasted until May 1951.

112. Relatively slow speed "shunts" or front end collisions were a cause of concern. It is fair to say that some of the postwar motormen weren't up to the standard of their prewar colleagues, and many drivers misjudged distances with results similar to those illustrated here.

113. Car 164 epitomises the latter years of the LUT, when very little was invested in new cars, and the trams that were on the road began to look antiquated.

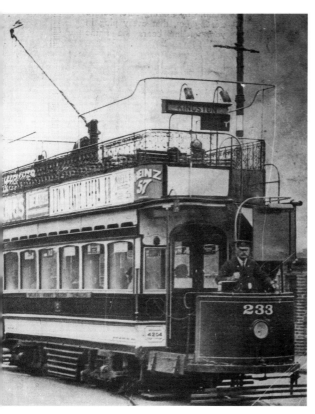

114. There was not even enough money to give each tram a top cover, and car 233 was fated to spend its whole operating life in more or less original condition. A further criticism of the LUT was that it was always overstocked with vehicles. Trams had been ordered in the early 1900s for extensions which never materialised.

115. Type U car 205 was renumbered 2362 by London Transport. The LUT's only concession to modernity was the "homemade" top cover.

116. The "Palace" cars of 1906 were the last word in contemporary tramcar design. Even in this 1931 view car 334 still radiates an air of solid reliability. Passenger comfort was not neglected and many type T trams received more comfortable seating in both saloons.

117. Car 2353 is seen in LT days when it will shortly be called upon to transport Boat Race crowds to and from Hammersmith. Note that it has received driver's windscreens, but still retains open balconies. As was usual in tramway operation, the motorman has raised the step and put a chain across the driving platform.

118. The LUT had one last trick up its sleeve, the UCC or Feltham type trams which were a revelation for passengers used to the "open air life" on the older cars. Operated on the Shepherds Bush to Uxbridge line, passenger totals soared, but this was too little too late, and ironically the tram's fate was sealed by another LUT experiment - the new trolleybuses.

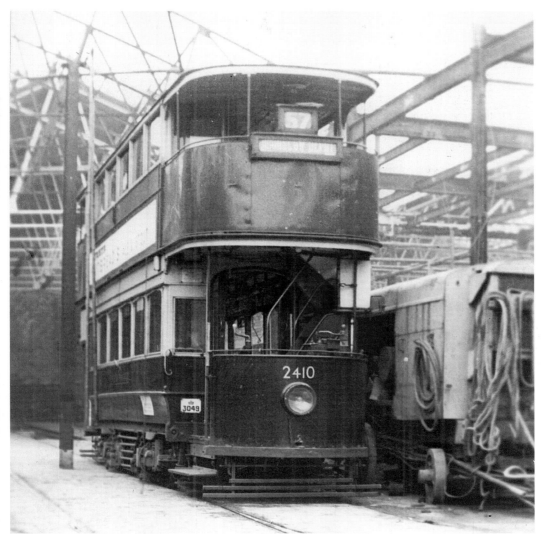

119. The funeral bell for the tramcar tolled in 1931, when the new LUT trolleybuses began to replace trams in the Kingston area. This photo gives a good comparison between the two electrically powered forms of transport.

120. Car 2410 (ex-LUT car 261) stands lonely sentinel, as Hounslow Depot is ripped apart in preparation for the replacing trolleybuses. This type WT car was scrapped in July 1936. Such was the melancholy fate of a once great tramway system.

Middleton Press

Easebourne Lane, Midhurst, W Sussex. GU29 9AZ Tel: 01730 813169 Fax: 01730 812601
*If books are not available from your local transport stockist, order direct with cheque,
Visa or Mastercard, post free UK.*

BRANCH LINES
Branch Line to Allhallows
Branch Line to Alton
Branch Lines around Ascot
Branch Line to Ashburton
Branch Lines around Bodmin
Branch Line to Bude
Branch Lines around Canterbury
Branch Lines around Chard & Yeovil
Branch Line to Cheddar
Branch Lines around Cromer
Branch Lines to Effingham Junction
Branch Lines around Exmouth
Branch Line to Fairford
Branch Lines around Gosport
Branch Line to Hawkhurst
Branch Line to Hayling
Branch Lines to Horsham
Branch Lines around Huntingdon
Branch Line to Ilfracombe
Branch Line to Kingswear
Branch Lines to Launceston & Princetown
Branch Lines to Longmoor
Branch Line to Looe
Branch Line to Lyme Regis
Branch Lines around March
Branch Lines around Midhurst
Branch Line to Minehead
Branch Line to Moretonhampstead
Branch Lines to Newport (IOW)
Branch Line to Padstow
Branch Lines around Plymouth
Branch Lines to Seaton and Sidmouth
Branch Line to Selsey
Branch Lines around Sheerness
Branch Line to Swanage *updated*
Branch Line to Tenterden
Branch Lines to Torrington
Branch Lines to Tunbridge Wells
Branch Line to Upwell
Branch Lines around Weymouth
Branch Lines around Wimborne
Branch Lines around Wisbech

NARROW GAUGE BRANCH LINES
Branch Line to Lynton
Branch Lines around Portmadoc 1923-46
Branch Lines around Porthmadog 1954-94
Two-Foot Gauge Survivors
Romneyrail

SOUTH COAST RAILWAYS
Ashford to Dover
Bournemouth to Weymouth
Brighton to Eastbourne
Chichester to Portsmouth
Dover to Ramsgate
Eastbourne to Hastings
Hastings to Ashford
Portsmouth to Southampton
Southampton to Bournemouth
Worthing to Chichester

SOUTHERN MAIN LINES
Basingstoke to Salisbury
Bromley South to Rochester
Charing Cross to Orpington
Crawley to Littlehampton
Dartford to Sittingbourne
East Croydon to Three Bridges
Epsom to Horsham
Exeter to Barnstaple

Exeter to Tavistock
Faversham to Dover
London Bridge to East Croydon
Orpington to Tonbridge
Tonbridge to Hastings
Salisbury to Yeovil
Swanley to Ashford
Tavistock to Plymouth
Victoria to East Croydon
Waterloo to Windsor
Waterloo to Woking
Woking to Portsmouth
Woking to Southampton
Yeovil to Exeter

EASTERN MAIN LINES
Fenchurch Street to Barking
Liverpool Street to Ilford

COUNTRY RAILWAY ROUTES
Andover to Southampton
Bath to Bristol
Bath to Evercreech Junction
Bournemouth to Evercreech Jn.
Burnham to Evercreech Junction
Croydon to East Grinstead
Didcot to Winchester
East Kent Light Railway
Fareham to Salisbury
Frome to Bristol
Guildford to Redhill
Porthmadog to Blaenau
Reading to Basingstoke
Reading to Guildford
Redhill to Ashford
Salisbury to Westbury
Stratford upon Avon to Cheltenham
Strood to Paddock Wood
Taunton to Barnstaple
Wenford Bridge to Fowey
Westbury to Bath
Woking to Alton
Yeovil to Dorchester

GREAT RAILWAY ERAS
Ashford from Steam to Eurostar
Clapham Junction 50 years of change
Festiniog in the Fifties
Festiniog in the Sixties
Isle of Wight Lines 50 years of change
Railways to Victory 1944-46
SECR Centenary album

LONDON SUBURBAN RAILWAYS
Caterham and Tattenham Corner
Charing Cross to Dartford
Clapham Jn. to Beckenham Jn.
East London Line
Finsbury Park to Alexandra Palace
Holborn Viaduct to Lewisham
Kingston and Hounslow Loops
Lewisham to Dartford
Lines around Wimbledon
London Bridge to Addiscombe
North London Line
South London Line
West Croydon to Epsom
West London Line
Willesden Junction to Richmond
Wimbledon to Epsom

STEAMING THROUGH
Steaming through Cornwall

Steaming through Kent
Steaming through West Hants
Steaming through West Sussex

TRAMWAY CLASSICS
Aldgate & Stepney Tramways
Barnet & Finchley Tramways
Bath Tramways
Bournemouth & Poole Tramways
Brighton's Tramways
Camberwell & W.Norwood Tramways
Clapham & Streatham Tramways
Dover's Tramways
East Ham & West Ham Tramways
Edgware and Willesden Tramways
Eltham & Woolwich Tramways
Embankment & Waterloo Tramways
Enfield & Wood Green Tramways
Exeter & Taunton Tramways
Gosport & Horndean Tramways
Greenwich & Dartford Tramways
Hammersmith & Hounslow Tramways
Hampstead & Highgate Tramways
Hastings Tramways
Holborn & Finsbury Tramways
Ilford & Barking Tramways
Kingston & Wimbledon Tramways
Lewisham & Catford Tramways
Liverpool Tramways 1. Eastern Routes
Liverpool Tramways 2. Southern Routes
Maidstone & Chatham Tramways
North Kent Tramways
Portsmouth's Tramways
Reading Tramways
Seaton & Eastbourne Tramways
Shepherds Bush & Uxbridge Tramways
Southampton Tramways
Southend-on-sea Tramways
Southwark & Deptford Tramways
Stamford Hill Tramways
Thanet's Tramways
Twickenham & Kingston Tramways
Victoria & Lambeth Tramways
Waltham Cross & Edmonton Tramways
Walthamstow & Leyton Tramways
Wandsworth & Battersea Tramways

TROLLEYBUS CLASSICS
Croydon Trolleybuses
Bournemouth Trolleybuses
Hastings Trolleybuses
Maidstone Trolleybuses
Reading Trolleybuses
Woolwich & Dartford Trolleybuses

WATERWAY ALBUMS
Kent and East Sussex Waterways
London to Portsmouth Waterway
Surrey Waterways
West Sussex Waterways

MILITARY BOOKS and VIDEO
Battle over Portsmouth
Battle over Sussex 1940
Blitz over Sussex 1941-42
Bombers over Sussex 1943-45
Bognor at War
Military Defence of West Sussex
Secret Sussex Resistance
Sussex Home Guard
War on the Line
War on the Line VIDEO

OTHER BOOKS
Betwixt Petersfield & Midhurst
Changing Midhurst
East Grinstead Then & Now
Garraway Father & Son
Index to all Stations
South Eastern & Chatham Railways
London Chatham & Dover Railway